Enrichment Book

Brian O'Doherty
Anne and Leonard Frobisher

gill & macmillan primary

Gill & Macmillan
Hume Avenue
Park West
Dublin 12
www.gillmacmillan.ie

ISBN: 978 07171 53794

Design: Design Image
Print origination: Carole Lynch
Internal illustrations: Kate Shannon and Sting Art
Technical drawings: MPS Limited
Consultant editor in mathematics curriculum and pedagogy: Betty Stoutt
Cover illustration: www.designbos.ie

The paper used in this book comes from the wood pulp of
managed forests. For every tree felled, at least one tree is
planted, thereby renewing natural resources.

Any links to external websites should not be construed as an endorsement
by Gill & Macmillan of the content or view of the linked material.

The publishers have made every effort to contact copyright holders
but any omissions will be rectified at the next reprint.

Unit		Strand	Page

*Access all Check-ups on our website, www.crackingmaths.ie

Practise!

1. Draw notation boards to show these numbers.
    a) 924   b) 3706   c) 4085   d) 603   e) 7159
    f) 8345   g) 14536   h) 27093   i) 30487   j) 41205

2. What is the value of the underlined digit in each of the following?
    a) 8956   b) 734   c) 6709   d) 12934   e) 16278
    f) 4763   g) 1976   h) 745   i) 26108   j) 32396
    k) 28719   l) 38195   m) 5386   n) 74002   o) 3801

3. Write these numbers in words.
    a) 378   b) 1594   c) 15719   d) 18004   e) 6812
    f) 21107   g) 5048   h) 36092   i) 45127   j) 6978

4. Work out the sequence and fill in the missing terms.
    a) 130, 180, 230, _____, _____, _____, _____
    b) 560, 535, _____, _____, 460, _____, _____, 385, _____
    c) 315, _____, 405, 450, _____, _____, 585, _____
    d) 830, 800, 760, 710, _____, _____, 500, _____, _____

5. Divide each of the following numbers by i) 10 and ii) 100.
    a) 14000   b) 9600   c) 17100   d) 21700   e) 5300
    f) 28500   g) 1900   h) 13900   i) 4000   j) 68700

6. Draw notation boards to represent each of these numbers.
    a) 2.59   b) 41.08   c) 35.96
    d) 70.4   e) 5.09   f) 36.8

7. In the following decimals, write down whether the underlined
    digit is a hundred, ten, unit, tenth or hundredth.
    a) 17.8   b) 26.37   c) 183.9   d) 39.27   e) 325.74
    f) 402.58   g) 4.56   h) 729.3   i) 309.26   j) 537.04

8. Round these numbers to the nearest ten.
    a) 13   b) 7   c) 48   d) 91   e) 98
    f) 112   g) 176   h) 234   i) 485   j) 703
    k) 987   l) 1432   m) 2029   n) 4714   o) 7836

9. Round these numbers to the nearest hundred.

   a) 63   b) 141   c) 268   d) 349   e) 786

   f) 935   g) 1170   h) 1552   i) 1826   j) 2347

   k) 2643   l) 3819   m) 4275   n) 6151   o) 9024

10. Round these numbers to the nearest thousand.

   a) 1723   b) 1496   c) 2089   d) 2502   e) 3389

   f) 4279   g) 5189   h) 7298   i) 8645   j) 9712

   k) 11934   l) 17459   m) 24523   n) 29268   o) 37500

Solve!   2. Place Value

Populations

Follow the clues to find the population of Bigville.

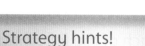

a) The population of Bigville is a 5-digit number.

b) The number uses the digits 3, 1, 4, 6 and 2, but not in that order.

c) The 6 has the smallest digit value.

d) The 4 is in the tens place.

e) The other 3 digits are in descending order.

Strategy hints!

1. Look for the important words in the question.

2. Think logically.

Extension

Follow the clues to find the population of Largedom.

a) The population of Largedom is a 5-digit number.

b) The number uses 5, 1, 4, 6 and 9, but not in that order.

c) The numbers in the thousands and hundreds places differ by 2.

d) The number in the thousands place is the 2nd highest digit.

e) The population will soon have 6 digits.

f) The last two digits are the 26th odd number.

1. Clara's Mystery Number

Clara has a mystery number.

She gives 3 clues to what her number could be.

My number has 4 different digits.

The unit digit is one half of the thousand digit.

The sum of the hundred and the ten digits is 9.

Lorna says, 'The mystery number is 4638.'

Copy Lorna's number.

Could what Lorna said be correct?

Explain why to a friend.

Investigate what Clara's mystery number could be.

2. Less Than Decimals

| 1 | 2 | 3 | 4 |

Fiona has 4 digit cards and a missing digits 'less than' statement.

0 • ☐ ☐ < 0 • ☐

Fiona uses 3 of her digit cards to complete the 'less than' statement.

0 • 3 1 < 0 • 4

Copy what Fiona did.

Is what she did correct?

Explain why to a friend.

Investigate ways of using 3 digit cards to complete the 'less than' statement correctly.

1. Estimate the answers to each of the following and then work out the answers to see how accurate your estimate was. Use your calculator to check your answers.

a)   195   b)   312   c)   1297   d)   2649   e)   2892   f)   4389
      306   289   704   1553   4307   514
  +   252   +   249   +   382   +   3998   +   2389   +   8478

g) €3987 + €2015 + €1489   h) €2895 + €6114 + €4555
i) € 8794 + €12108 + €16368   j) €13598 + €19703 + €26485

2. Estimate the answers to these and then work out the answers to see how accurate your estimate was. Use your calculator to check your answers.

a)   4702 b)   7289 c)   9001 d)   13123 e)   19806 f)   27743
   − 2893   − 3492   − 6794   −   8697   − 14588   − 24829

g) 8521 − 2768   h) 6014 − 1287   i) 7624 − 3857
j) 15732 − 9189   k) 23118 − 17756   l) 37483 − 28647

Counting the Coast

3. The following table shows the populations of 4 different towns as recorded in the census of 2008 and the census of 2013.

Town	Population 2008	Population 2013
Bayview	12248	11729
Harbourville	8578	11684
Oceantown	10194	14375
Seapoint	16932	12267

a) Which town had the greatest population increase from 2008 to 2013?

b) What was the size of that increase?

c) Which town had the greatest population decrease from 2008 to 2013?

d) What was the size of that decrease?

e) What was the combined population of Harbourville and Oceantown in 2013?

f) What was the combined population of Bayview and Seapoint in 2008?

g) What was the difference between the population of Bayview and Harbourville in 2008 and 2013?

h) How has that difference changed over the 5 years?

i) What was the total population of the 4 towns in 2008 and 2013?

j) What is the difference between the total population of the 4 towns in 2008 and 2013?

Solve!
3. Operations I

Lost Marbles

Ralph has lost his marbles.

Shauna said, 'I found them. I kept 12 and gave the rest to Tomas.'

Tomas said, 'I kept 11 and gave the rest to Una.'

Una said, 'I lost 10 but I have 6 left.'

How many marbles did Shauna give to Tomas?

Strategy hints!

1. Look for the important words in the question.

2. Have a go.

3. Work backwards.

Extension

Make up more problems like this one. See if a classmate can work them out.

1. Máire's Book

Máire chooses a book from the library.

She flicks through the book to make a visual estimate of the number of words there could be for her to read.

Máire says, 'I estimate that there are 18342 words in my book.'

Is Máire's estimate a sensible one? Explain why to a friend.

Máire decides to check her estimate.

She finds that her book has 134 pages and that on 1 page there are 127 words.

Use what Máire found to calculate a reasonable estimate of the number of words in her book.

Explain to a friend how you worked it out.

> Investigate estimating the number of words in different books in your library.

2. Two 2s and Two 3s

Natasha has a challenge for her friends.

She makes a decimal addition with 6 missing digits and with an answer of 22.33.

She challenges her friends to work out the missing digits.

Ella says that this is a possible solution.

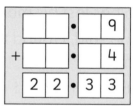

Complete what Ella did.

Is what Ella did correct?

Explain why to a friend.

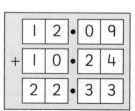

> Investigate other ways of completing Natasha's addition correctly.

1. Write down each of the odd numbers in this list of numbers.

49	28	11	37	64	8
65	40	23	86	99	104

2. Write down the even numbers in the following list of numbers.

52	70	7	23	48	19
31	96	85	14	63	117

3. Write down the numbers on the following list that are prime numbers.

19	15	21	37	9	41
55	53	67	91	29	110

4. Write down the numbers on the following list that are not prime numbers.

11	28	35	43	7	51
33	61	49	36	81	13

5. List all of the factors of the following numbers.

a) 12　　b) 16　　c) 27　　d) 32　　e) 20　　f) 42

6. Find the common factors of the following pairs of numbers.

a) 9 and 12　　　　b) 12 and 20　　　　c) 16 and 24

d) 18 and 30　　　　e) 27 and 36　　　　f) 28 and 42

7. List the first 8 multiples of the following numbers.

a) 4　　b) 9　　c) 5　　d) 7　　e) 6　　f) 12

8. True or false?

    a) 364 is a multiple of 7   b) 428 is a multiple of 6

    c) 295 is a multiple of 3   d) 736 is a multiple of 8

    e) 513 is a multiple of 9   f) 658 is a multiple of 12

Solve!   4. Number Theory 1

Closest Five

In a counting game, if a number is a multiple of 5, or next to a multiple of 5, it is thrown out.

You must count like this:

1, 2, 3, 7, 8, 12, 13 ...

What is the 25th number you will count?

Extension

All the numbers you don't count up to 50 are put into a hat.
How many of these numbers do not end in a 9?

Strategy hints!

1. Look for the important words in the question.

2. Look for a pattern.

3. Try an easier problem.

1. Totals Are Odd Numbers

Molly has 9 number cards
and a blank 3×3 grid.

| 1 | 2 | 3 | 4 | 5 |

| 6 | 7 | 8 | 9 |

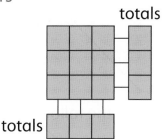

totals

Molly tries to put her 9 numbers into the
grid so that the total of each row and of each
column is an odd number.

This is what Molly did.

Copy what Molly did.

Complete the 6 totals.

How many of the 6
totals are odd numbers?

Explain to your friend how you decided.

totals

3	6	1
2	5	4
8	7	9

totals

> Investigate
> making as many
> odd row and odd
> column totals as
> you can.

2. Which Numbers?

Lauryn has 5 number cards.

| 2 | 3 | 4 | 5 | 6 |

She chooses 2 of her number cards.

| 2 | 3 |

Lauryn says, '2 and 3 are factors of these 3 numbers.'

| 12 | 24 | 6 |

Is what Lauryn said correct?

Explain why to a friend.

Find 4 more numbers for Lauryn
which have 2 and 3
as their factors.

Explain to your friend how you decided.

> Investigate using 2 of
> Lauryn's number cards
> to find numbers of which
> they are factors.

1. Identify these lines by writing the correct name for each.

   a)   b)   c)   d)   e)

2. Are the following angles acute, obtuse, reflex, straight or right?

   a)   b)   c)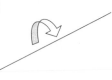

   d) 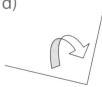   e)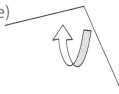

3. Name the angle in each of the following (acute, right, obtuse, straight, reflex angle or full rotation).

   a) 238°   b) 90°   c) 109°   d) 78°

   e) 180°   f) 14°   g) 360°   h) 96°

4. Estimate the size of each of these angles and then check your estimate by measuring them using your protractor.

   a)   b)   c)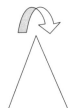

   d)    e)

5. Draw these angles using a pencil, ruler and protractor.

   a) 30°   b) 140°   c) 65°   d) 95°

   e) 80°   f) 165°   g) 110°   h) 45°

6. Work out the missing angles in each of these triangles.

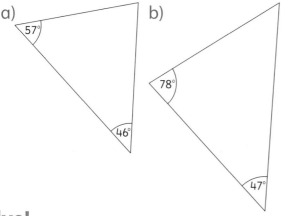

a)   57°   46°

b)   78°   47°

c)   63°   99°

Solve!

Letter Angle

The angle formed where the arms of the capital letter L meet is called a right angle.

a) Two capital letters in the first 8 letters of the alphabet each contain 4 right angles. Find both of these letters.

b) What is the last capital letter of the alphabet to contain 2 right angles within it?

c) Find as many items as you can in your classroom that contain right angles.

Strategy hints!

1. Look for the important words in the question.

2. Use a drawing.

3. Make a model.

Extension

The angle formed where the arms of the capital letter A meet is less than a right angle.

Find the capital letters of the alphabet that contain at least 1 angle that is smaller than a right angle.

1. Jane's Angles

Jane draws 3 different kinds of angle on 3×3 dotty grids.

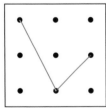 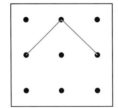 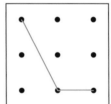

Copy what Jane did.

Jane says, 'One of my angles is a right angle, another is an acute angle and the other is an obtuse angle.' Is what Jane said correct?

Investigate drawing right, acute and obtuse angles on 3×3 dotty grids.

Explain why to a friend.

Write right, acute or obtuse for each angle in your copy.

2. Gerard's Clock

Gerard has a 12-hour analogue clock.

Copy the drawing of the clock and draw the time that Gerard's clock shows.

Explain to a friend how you did this.

Write the time that Gerard's clock shows.

Explain how you decided to your friend.

Gerard says, 'The angle made by the 2 hands of Gerard's clock is 120 degrees.'

Is what Gerard said correct?

Explain why to your friend.

Investigate the angles made by the 2 hands on a clock when showing half-hour times.

1. Complete these number sentences by filling in the missing sign
    (+ − × ÷).

    a) 196 ⬚ 14 = 14

    b) 207 ⬚ 149 = 58

    c) 27 ⬚ 36 = 972

    d) 138 ⬚ 179 = 317

    e) 374 ⬚ 185 = 189

    f) 364 ⬚ 13 = 28

2. Make these word problems into number sentences and then solve
    them. You can use your calculator.

    a) Claire bought 19 trays of marigolds. Each tray has 12 flowers
        in it. How many flowers did she buy altogether?

    b) In St Patrick's Primary School, there are 755 pupils. If 468 of the
        pupils are girls, how many boys are there in the school?

    c) If there are 384 players participating in a basketball
        tournament with 24 teams, how many players are there in
        each squad?

    d) If 67 cars parked in a car park on Monday, 79 cars parked
        there on Tuesday, 58 cars on Wednesday and 86 cars
        on Thursday, how many cars were parked in the car park
        over the course of the 4 days?

3. Use your calculator to solve these equations. Write your answers in your copy.

a) $37 \times \underline{\hspace{1cm}} = 4995$

b) $3482 + \underline{\hspace{1cm}} = 7083$

c) $\frac{1}{8}$ of $872 = \underline{\hspace{1cm}}$

d) $\underline{\hspace{1cm}} - 3659 = 2594$

e) $2987 - \underline{\hspace{1cm}} = 879$

f) $\underline{\hspace{1cm}} \div 29 = 187$

g) $7.28 \times 0.6 = \underline{\hspace{1cm}}$

h) 75% of $\underline{\hspace{1cm}} = 726$

4. Make up word problems for the following number sentences.

a) $48 \div 6 =$

b) $924 - 458 =$

c) $187 + 269 + 328 =$

d) $45 \times 28 =$

Solve!   6. Equations

Different Numbers

A and B are 2 different numbers. Both are less than 10.

$(A \times A) + (B \times B) = 34$

A is smaller than B.

What numbers are A and B?

Strategy hints!

1. Look for the important words in the question.
2. Have a go.
3. Think logically.

Extension

J and K are 2 different numbers. Both are less than 10.

J is smaller than K.

$J + K$ is 14 less than $J \times K$.

1. A Visit to the Cinema

For her birthday, Andrea visits a cinema with 5 of her friends.

Andrea writes a problem about her visit.

Six of us each bought a cone of popcorn at the cinema. Each cone of popcorn cost €3.95.

What was the total cost of the popcorn?

Write the number sentence for Andrea's problem.

Work out the answer.

Explain to a friend how you worked it out.

> Investigate writing maths problems about a visit of 6 children to a cinema.

2. Dillon's Equations

Dillon has 4 equations to solve.

$$€6.16 + €\boxed{} = €9$$

$$€\boxed{} \times 5 = €30.80$$

$$€6.16 - €\boxed{} = €4.30$$

$$€\boxed{} \div 4 = €1.54$$

Copy Dillon's equations.

Work out the missing numbers.

Explain to a friend how you did each one.

> Investigate writing 2 maths problems for each equation.

1. How many seconds are in each of the following?
    a) 1 min 47 sec   b) 2 mins 28 sec   c) 3 mins 36 sec
    d) 4 mins 53 sec   e) 7 mins 12 sec   f) 5 mins 9 sec
    g) 6 mins 54 sec   h) 9 mins 49 sec

2. How many minutes are in each of the following?
    a) 1 hour 25 mins   b) 1 hour 54 mins   c) 3 hours 37 mins
    d) 2 hours 18 mins   e) 5 hours 46 mins   f) 9 hours 2 mins
    g) 6 hours 57 mins   h) 8 hours 24 mins

3. a) hrs mins   b) hrs mins   c) hrs mins   d) hrs mins
          4   38   5   28   4   36   7   48
      + 3   16   + 1   27   + 2   39   + 1   29

    e) hrs mins   f) hrs mins   g) hrs mins   h) hrs mins
          2   27   1   53   3   29   6   47
          1   32   4   17   2   38   1   29
      + 3   18   + 3   26   + 4   16   + 5   35

    i) hrs mins   j) hrs mins   k) hrs mins   l) hrs mins
          5   42   6   13   7   05   9   23
      − 2   27   − 4   49   − 3   56   − 6   38

    m) hrs mins   n) hrs mins   o) hrs mins   p) hrs mins
          7   15   8   31   6   26   9   44
      − 4   29   − 7   38   − 1   47   − 7   58

4. Here is the plan for a Fun Day.

Time	Event
11:30	Teddy Bear's Picnic
12:10	Novelty Games
12:45	Face Painting
13:40	Treasure Hunt
14:25	Live DJ
15:00	Raffle
15:25	Finale
15:40	Clean Up

a) How long did the Face Painting last?
b) How much time was there from the end of the Novelty Games until the Live DJ started?
c) What was the combined time spent on the Teddy Bear's Picnic and Novelty Games?
d) How much longer did the Treasure Hunt last than the Live DJ?
e) What is the total duration of the Fun Day up to the Clean Up?

Future Time

I am thinking of a date next year.

It is more than 40 but less than 80 days after New Year's Day.

The month and day of the month are both even numbers.

The digits in the day of the month add up to 5.

What date am I thinking of?

Strategy hints!

1. Look for the important words in the question.
2. Use a table or a chart.

Extension

I am thinking of a date next year.

It is more than 35 but less than 60 days before New Year's Day.

The month and day of the month are both odd 2-digit numbers.

The day of the month and the month when multiplied together give a number less than 125.

What date am I thinking of?

1. Planning a Football Match

Eoin plans the times when his school football team can play their matches.

Each match has 2 halves of 30 minutes each.

Between the 2 halves there is an interval of 10 minutes.

Matches are played in the morning after 9:15am and end before lunchtime, or after lunchtime and finish before school ends.

A match always starts on the hour, quarter past, quarter to, or half past the hour.

Jodie says, 'A match could start at 10:30am and finish at 12 o'clock just in time for lunch.' Could what Jodie said be correct?

Explain why to a friend.

> Investigate when matches could be played in your school using Eoin's plans.

2. Mirror Times

Sinéad has a 24-hour digital clock.

Copy Sinéad's time on the clock.

What is the am or pm time on Sinéad's clock?

Explain why to a friend.

Sinéad notices two Mirror Times that occur on her clock.

Copy the times.

What are the am or pm times of Sinéad's Mirror Times?

Explain to your friend why these two times might be called Mirror Times.

> Investigate other Mirror Times on a 24-hour digital clock.

1. Try these. Check that your answers are equivalent to the original fractions.

a) $\dfrac{1 \times 3}{3 \times 3} =$ ___ = ___

b) $\dfrac{3 \times 2}{4 \times 2} =$ ___ = ___

c) $\dfrac{2 \times 4}{3 \times 4} =$ ___ = ___

d) $\dfrac{1 \times 3}{6 \times 3} =$ ___ = ___

e) $\dfrac{2 \times 2}{5 \times 2} =$ ___ = ___

f) $\dfrac{7 \times 3}{10 \times 3} =$ ___ = ___

2. Now find equivalent fractions for the following fractions by multiplying by a member of the family of 1.

a) $\frac{1}{4}$
b) $\frac{3}{8}$
c) $\frac{5}{6}$
d) $\frac{4}{7}$

e) $\frac{7}{9}$
f) $\frac{3}{10}$
g) $\frac{4}{5}$
h) $\frac{11}{12}$

3. Try these. Check that your answers are equivalent to the original fractions.

a) $\dfrac{4}{6} \div \dfrac{2}{2} =$ ___

b) $\dfrac{9}{12} \div \dfrac{3}{3} =$ ___

c) $\dfrac{12}{16} \div \dfrac{4}{4} =$ ___

d) $\dfrac{12}{15} \div \dfrac{3}{3} =$ ___

e) $\dfrac{14}{16} \div \dfrac{2}{2} =$ ___

f) $\dfrac{36}{42} \div \dfrac{6}{6} =$ ___

g) $\dfrac{32}{40} \div \dfrac{8}{8} =$ ___

h) $\dfrac{49}{56} \div \dfrac{7}{7} =$ ___

i) $\dfrac{45}{63} \div \dfrac{9}{9} =$ ___

4. Now find equivalent fractions for the following fractions by dividing by a member of the family of 1.

a) $\frac{27}{30}$
b) $\frac{15}{25}$
c) $\frac{16}{24}$
d) $\frac{28}{35}$

e) $\frac{64}{72}$
f) $\frac{36}{40}$
g) $\frac{30}{42}$
h) $\frac{36}{48}$

Paper Fold

Gemma folded a piece of paper in half.
Then she folded that half in half.
Then she folded it in half again.
She then opened up the piece of paper.

a) How many little rectangles were on the opened piece of paper?

b) Gemma has turned her piece of paper into many smaller equal pieces by her folding. How could this be written as a fraction that is equal to 1 whole?

Strategy hints!

1. Look for the important words in the question.
2. Look for a pattern.
3. Make a model.

Extension

a) Look at 1 half of the unfolded sheet. What fractional name for 1 half has Gemma's folding made?

b) Look at 1 quarter of the unfolded sheet. What fractional name for 1 quarter has Gemma's folding made?

1. Which Are Equivalent?

Ciara has 12 number cards and a blank equivalent proper fractions statement.

Ciara completes the equivalent fractions statement using 4 of her number cards.

This is what she did.

| 1 | 2 | 3 | 4 | 5 | 6 |
| 7 | 8 | 9 | 10 | 11 | 12 |

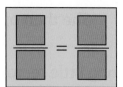

$$\frac{1}{2} = \frac{3}{6}$$

Copy Ciara's statement.

Is what Ciara did correct?

Explain why to a friend.

> Investigate other ways of completing Ciara's statement correctly.

2. Colm's Proper Fractions

Colm has 6 number cards.

| 1 | 2 | 3 | 4 | 5 | 6 |

He starts to make as many proper fractions as possible. Each time he makes a proper fraction, he uses 2 of his 6 number cards. Here are 2 that he made.

$$\frac{3}{6} \qquad \frac{2}{3}$$

Copy what Colm did.

Is what he did correct?

Explain why to a friend.

Make as many different proper fractions for Colm as you can, each time using 2 of the 6 number cards.

> Investigate sorting your fractions into those less than $\frac{1}{2}$, equal to $\frac{1}{2}$ and greater than $\frac{1}{2}$.

1. Identify each of the following 2-D shapes from the list in question 2.

a)   b)   c)   d)   e)

f)   g)   h)   i)   j)

2. Copy this table in your copybook, then sort this list of 2-D shapes into the table.

    circle, parallelogram, rectangle, equilateral triangle, hexagon, rhombus, square, scalene triangle, pentagon, isosceles triangle

Polygon	Regular Polygon	Other

3. The following is the description of a triangle – what kind of triangle is it?

    a) It has 3 sides.

    b) All sides are equal.

    c) All angles are equal.

4. Draw a square, a rectangle, an equilateral triangle and an isosceles triangle in your copy and then draw in the lines of symmetry on each.

5. Do pentagons tessellate? Draw 5 pentagons to prove that your answer is right.

6. Identify which of these letters are symmetrical. Write your answer in your copy.

A V Z E L I M

Solve! 10. 2-D Shapes

Balancing Act

a) Does the square have the same mass as the triangle?

b) Is it heavier than the triangle or is it lighter than the triangle?

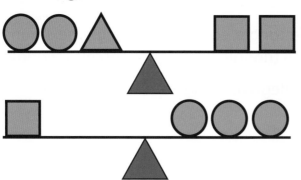

Strategy hints!

1. Look for the important words in the question.
2. Use a drawing.
3. Think logically.

Extension

How many circles will balance with 2 triangles?

1. Alison's Quadrilaterals

Alison has lots of 3×3 dotty grids.

She draws a quadrilateral on 3 of her dotty grids.

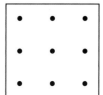

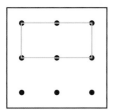 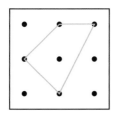 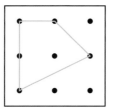

Copy Alison's 3 quadrilaterals.

Explain to a friend how you did them.

For each quadrilateral, write about its sides and its angles.

> Investigate drawing different quadrilaterals on 3x3 dotty grids.

2. Niall's Symmetrical Polygons

Niall has 3 yellow and 3 blue 5cm equilateral triangles.

He uses all 6 of his triangles to make a symmetrical polygon.

Copy and colour Niall's polygon.

How many sides has Niall's polygon?

What is the perimeter of Niall's polygon?

Explain to a friend how you worked it out.

How many angles has Niall's polygon?

What are the sizes of each angle?

Explain to your friend how you worked them out.

Draw a line of symmetry of Niall's polygon.

Explain to your friend how you decided where it should be drawn.

> Investigate making other symmetrical polygons with the 6 triangles.

1. Estimate the answers before multiplying. Then check your answers with a calculator.

   a) 167   b) 146   c) 129   d) 163   e) 215   f) 185
      ×   8   × 12   × 17   × 26   × 24   × 32

   g) 278   h) 326   i) 374   j) 346   k) 172   l) 149
      × 29   × 37   × 18   × 28   × 36   × 27

2. Estimate the answers to each of the following and then work out the answers.

   a) 7|182   b) 9|261   c) 11|198

   d) 8|280   e) 12|468   f) 6|534

3. Now try these. **Remember:** there could be remainders.

   a) 1272 ÷ 8   b) 1968 ÷ 6   c) 4605 ÷ 12   d) 2943 ÷ 4
   e) 6280 ÷ 10   f) 3843 ÷ 7   g) 8439 ÷ 5   h) 7564 ÷ 11
   i) 6687 ÷ 9   j) 5456 ÷ 8   k) 3897 ÷ 7   l) 4930 ÷ 5

4. Try these by estimating first and then trying your estimates in the multiplication questions.

   a) 16 × ____ = 112   b) 18 × ____ = 90   c) 24 × ____ = 192
   d) 28 × ____ = 168   e) 35 × ____ = 315   f) 39 × ____ = 156

5. Now try these. (Hint: none of the answers are bigger than 9.)

   a) 112 ÷ 14   b) 153 ÷ 17   c) 138 ÷ 23
   d) 189 ÷ 27   e) 180 ÷ 36   f) 384 ÷ 48

6. Now try these and find the remainder by subtracting.

   a) 163 ÷ 18   b) 214 ÷ 25   c) 296 ÷ 38
   d) 307 ÷ 46   e) 468 ÷ 57   f) 617 ÷ 83

7. Now try these. **Remember:** the first part of your answer will be in the tens column, so you will be estimating by multiplying by a 10 (there could be remainders).

   a) 208 ÷ 13   b) 648 ÷ 24   c) 537 ÷ 29

   d) 768 ÷ 32   e) 703 ÷ 37   f) 939 ÷ 41

8. Share a prize of €938 equally among 14 people.

9. If 26 jelly beans are in each packet and there are 965 jelly beans in total, how many packets of jelly beans can be filled and how many will be left over?

Solve!   11. Operations 2

Short Cut

Find the quick way to answer this problem:

1234 × 9 − 1234 × 8

Strategy hints!
1. Look for the important words in the question.
2. Try an easier problem.

Extension

Find the quick way to answer this problem:

6420 × 10 − 199

1. Emily's Difference

Emily has 8 digit cards and 2 missing digits decimal multiplications.

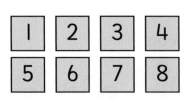

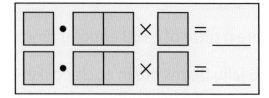

She tries to use all 8 of her digit cards to complete the 2 multiplications so that the difference between their answers is as small as possible.

This is what Emily did.

| 1 • 8 5 × 4 = ____ |
| 2 • 6 7 × 3 = ____ |

Copy what Emily did.

Work out the answers.

Explain to a friend how you worked them out.

What is the difference between the 2 answers?

Explain to your friend how you worked this out.

> Investigate ways of making the difference between the 2 answers as small as possible.

2. Rachael's Puzzle

Rachael sets a puzzle for her friend Paul.

This is what Rachael said to Paul, with space for Paul to write his answers.

Rachael	**Paul**
Think of a 3-digit number.	372
Write the number twice to make a 6-digit number with the last digits as 3 decimal places.	372.372
Divide your number by 7.	....
Divide your answer by 11.	....
Divide your last answer by 13.	....
What number did you end with?	....

Copy Rachael's instructions.

Copy and complete what Paul did.

Explain to a friend how you did this.

Investigate following Rachael's instructions with different 3-digit starter numbers.

1. When you roll a die, what are the chances of the following happening?
   a) Rolling any individual number
   b) Rolling an odd number
   c) Rolling a multiple of 3
   d) Rolling a multiple of 2
   e) Rolling a prime number

2. Put all the kings, queens and jacks from every suit into a bag. If you were to pick 1 card out of the bag, what are the chances of it being:
   a) a queen?
   b) a red king?
   c) the jack of spades?

3. If you were to pick 2 cards from the same bag as above, what are the chances of 1 of them being:
   a) a black jack?
   b) an ace of any colour?

4. Play 10 rounds of rock, paper, scissors with a friend and record the result in a table in your copy like the one below.

Round	Your Name	Your Friend's Name
1	✓	
2		✓
3		✓
4		
5		

Round	Your Name	Your Friend's Name
6		
7		
8		
9		
10		

a) Were the results as you expected them to be?

b) Is it a fair/random way of deciding an outcome?

5. Now try it again. This time record in the table what object each person chose in each round. Check to see if there is a pattern.

6. What are the chances of the following happening?

a) Guessing the day on which someone was born ____ in ____ chance.

b) Rolling a die and getting a prime number is a ____ in ____ chance.

c) Picking a vowel from a bag of letters of the alphabet is a ____ in ____ chance.

d) Picking the ace of spades from a deck of playing cards is a ____ in ____ chance.

Card Shuffle

10 cards are numbered
1 to 10.

Shuffling Sammy deals out the
cards 2, 4 and 7.

a) If the next card is an even number, you win a prize. What is the chance that the next card will be an even number?

b) If the next card is 5 or bigger, you lose. What is the chance that the next card will be 5 or bigger?

Strategy hints!

1. Look for the important words in the question.
2. Use a drawing.
3. Think logically.

Extension

Shuffling Sammy takes 20 cards. There are 2 of each number from 1 to 10.

He turns over 3, 5 and 10.

What is the chance of the next card being odd and bigger than 4?

1. Daniel's Spinner

Daniel has a blank spinner.

He also has 12 number stickers to put on his spinner.

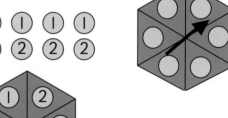

Daniel chooses 6 of his number stickers to put on the spinner.

Copy Daniel's completed spinner.

Daniel spins the arrow on his spinner. Is the chance of the arrow landing on the number 1 impossible, unlikely, even, likely or certain?

Explain how you decided to a friend.

> Investigate choosing different sets of 6 number stickers for the spinner.

2. Jack's Number Cards

Jack has 4 red and 4 blue number cards.

He puts his cards face down into a red pack and a blue pack. Then he shuffles both packs separately.

Jack picks the top card in each pack and gets a 1 and a 1.

Copy and complete this statement for Jack.

The product of ⬛1 and ①1 is ☐ .

Jack says, 'The chance of getting 2 cards with this product is 1 in 16.'

Is what Jack said true or false?

Explain why to a friend.

> Investigate the chances of getting different products of 2 cards chosen from the red and blue packs.

1. Try these. **Remember:** only add the numerators.

   a) $\frac{1}{3} + \frac{1}{3}$

   b) $\frac{1}{6} + \frac{5}{6}$

   c) $\frac{3}{7} + \frac{2}{7}$

   d) $\frac{4}{9} + \frac{3}{9}$

   e) $\frac{7}{10} + \frac{3}{10}$

   f) $\frac{6}{11} + \frac{3}{11}$

2. From the size of the fractions, see if you can estimate what the answers will be.

   a) $\frac{1}{2} + \frac{1}{4}$

   b) $\frac{1}{3} + \frac{1}{2}$

   c) $\frac{1}{4} + \frac{1}{6}$

   d) $\frac{3}{8} + \frac{1}{2}$

3. Now try these. Remember to change the fractions so that they have the same denominator. Estimate the answers first.

   a) $\frac{1}{2} + \frac{1}{6}$

   b) $\frac{1}{5} + \frac{1}{10}$

   c) $\frac{1}{4} + \frac{1}{8}$

   d) $\frac{1}{6} + \frac{1}{12}$

   e) $\frac{1}{4} + \frac{1}{6}$

   f) $\frac{1}{6} + \frac{1}{8}$

4. Try these and write your answers both ways.

   a) $\frac{3}{4} + \frac{2}{3}$

   b) $\frac{2}{3} + \frac{5}{6}$

   c) $\frac{3}{4} + \frac{5}{8}$

   d) $\frac{7}{8} + \frac{5}{6}$

   e) $\frac{4}{9} + \frac{5}{6}$

   f) $\frac{2}{3} + \frac{4}{5}$

5. Now try these. Remember to change the whole into the relevant member of the family of 1.

   a) $1 - \frac{4}{7}$

   b) $1 - \frac{1}{6}$

   c) $1 - \frac{3}{8}$

   d) $1 - \frac{2}{5}$

   e) $1 - \frac{7}{10}$

   f) $1 - \frac{5}{12}$

6. See if you can work these out. Remember to find the LCM of the denominators so that you can make equivalent fractions with the same denominator.

   a) $\frac{7}{8} - \frac{1}{4}$

   b) $\frac{7}{9} - \frac{2}{3}$

   c) $\frac{11}{12} - \frac{5}{6}$

   d) $\frac{3}{4} - \frac{2}{3}$

   e) $\frac{4}{5} - \frac{3}{4}$

   f) $\frac{8}{9} - \frac{5}{6}$

7. A glass of orange juice was $\frac{7}{8}$ full. If Bob drank $\frac{2}{3}$ of the juice, what fraction of the juice was left?

8.  Jenny skipped for $\frac{4}{5}$ of a kilometre and then she hopped for a further $\frac{2}{3}$ of a kilometre. How far did she travel in total?

Busy Bus

A busy bus picked up 40 people at the depot.

At the shops, $\frac{1}{4}$ of the people got off and 4 got on.

At the library, $\frac{1}{2}$ of the people got off and 7 got on.

a) How many people were on the bus after the library?

b) $\frac{1}{3}$ of the people left on the bus were school students. How many school students were on the bus?

Strategy hints!

1. Look for the important words in the question.
2. Have a go.
3. Work backwards.

Extension

The next day, the same bus picked up 60 people at the depot.

At the shops, $\frac{1}{4}$ of the people got off and 5 got on.

At the library, $\frac{1}{2}$ of the people got off and 8 got on.

a) How many people were on the bus after the library?

b) One more than $\frac{1}{3}$ of the people on the bus were school students. There were 3 female students to every male student. How many male students were on the bus?

1. Philip's Fraction Shapes

Philip has 7 fraction shapes.

He puts 3 of his fraction shapes together to make an addition of 3 fractions.

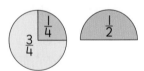

Make a copy of what Philip did.

Explain to a friend how you did this.

Philip writes the fraction addition in symbols.

$$\frac{3}{4} + \frac{1}{4} + \frac{1}{2} = \underline{\hspace{2cm}}$$

Copy Philip's fraction addition.

Work out the answer as a mixed number.

Explain to your friend how you did this.

> Investigate other additions Philip could make using his fraction shapes.

2. Less Than One Half

Louise has 7 fraction cards.

| $\frac{1}{8}$ | $\frac{1}{4}$ | $\frac{3}{8}$ | $\frac{1}{2}$ | $\frac{5}{8}$ | $\frac{3}{4}$ | $\frac{7}{8}$ |

She chooses 2 of her fraction cards to make a subtraction with an answer less than $\frac{1}{2}$.

$$\frac{5}{8} - \frac{3}{8} = \underline{\hspace{1.5cm}}$$

Copy Louise's subtraction.

Work out the answer for Louise.

Is the answer less than $\frac{1}{2}$?

Explain why to a friend.

>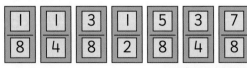
> Investigate using Louise's fraction cards to make subtractions with answers less than $\frac{1}{2}$.

1. Use a sieve of Eratosthenes to identify if the following numbers are prime.

   a) 27   b) 19   c) 31   d) 53   e) 57   f) 81

2. Check to see if these numbers can be arranged into rectangular shapes (for example, $8 = 2$ rows of 4).

   a) 9   b) 13   c) 21   d) 27   e) 23   f) 33

3. See how many different ways you can arrange the following numbers into rectangular shapes.

   a) 18   b) 24   c) 20   d) 32   e) 36   f) 40

4. Work out what these square numbers could be.
   a) What is the 4th square number?
   b) What is the 6th square number?
   c) What is the 9th square number?
   d) What is the 11th square number?
   e) What is the 15th square number?
   f) What is the 23rd square number?

5. Write these as multiplication sentences and then work out the answers.

   a) 5^2 b) 8^2 c) 16^2 d) 24^2 e) 29^2 f) 38^2

1. Boys and Girls

All of the students at our school stood in a long line for a photo.

We stood in groups of 4: boy, then girl, then girl, then boy, all the way to the end of the line.

Which of these statements is true?

a)   From the start of the line, the girls are in the 4 times table pattern.

b)   There is always a boy with a girl on either side of him.

c)   The 16th in line is a girl.

d)   From the start of the line, the boys are in the 4 times table pattern.

> **Strategy hints!**
> 1.   Look for the important words in the question.
> 2.   Look for a pattern.
> 3.   Use a drawing.

Extension

a)   Will the 100th student be a boy or a girl?

b)   Will the 147th student be a boy or a girl?

2. Pattern Maker

A pattern maker made the following pattern:

odd, odd, even, even, odd, odd, even, even …

The numbers he used were:

1, 3, 4, 6, 7, 9, 10, 12 …

a)   Find the 6th number the pattern maker had to skip in order to make this pattern.

b)   What is the 20th number that the pattern maker used?

> **Strategy hints!**
> 1.   Look for the important words in the question.
> 2.   Look for a pattern.
> 3.   Think logically.

Extension

Up to 100, how many numbers would the pattern maker have to skip in order to make this pattern?

1. Consecutive Prime Numbers

Maria lists the sequence of prime numbers.

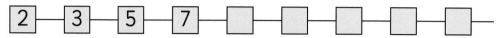

Complete and extend Maria's sequence.

Explain to a friend how you did this.

Maria notices that the sum of the 3 consecutive prime numbers 5, 7 and 11 is also a

$$\boxed{5} + \boxed{7} + \boxed{11} = \underline{}$$

prime number. Copy Maria's addition and work out the answer. Explain to your friend how you did this.

Is what Maria noticed about the answer being a prime number always true, sometimes true or never true?

Explain how you decided to your friend.

> Investigate sums of 3 consecutive prime numbers.

2. Factors of Square Numbers

Tadhg lists the sequence of square numbers.

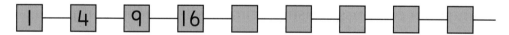

Complete and extend Tadhg's sequence.

Explain to a friend how you did this.

Tadhg inspects the square number 9 for its factors. He says, 'The factors of 9 are 1, 3 and 9. So 9 has 3 factors.'

Is what Tadhg said correct?

Explain how you decided to your friend.

> Investigate what is special about the number of factors of square numbers.

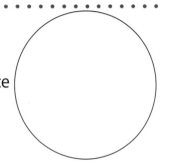

1. Draw a circle in your copy and label the following parts with these labels.

   radius   diameter   circumference

2. What's the relationship between a radius and a diameter?

3. Draw this table in your copy and fill in the blanks.

	Radius	Diameter
Circle A	14cm	
Circle B		32cm
Circle C		43cm
Circle D	27.5cm	
Circle E	48.5m	
Circle F		113cm

4. Using your compass, construct circles with the following radii.

   a) 6cm   b) 3.5cm   c) 5.5cm

5. Using your compass, construct circles with the following diameters.

   a) 10cm   b) 14cm   c) 13cm

6. Do circles tessellate? Draw an example of this in your copy to prove your answer.

Golf Score

The last time I played golf, my score was a 3-digit number.

All 3 digits were different.

The 3 digits added up to 11.

My score was the smallest possible number to fit these clues.

a) What was my score?

b) My 2 friends made the second smallest and the third smallest scores that fit these clues. What were my friends' scores?

c) How much did I beat them by?

Strategy hints!

1. Look for the important words in the question.

2. Think logically.

Extension

The next time I played golf, my score was a 3-digit number.

All 3 digits were different and the 3 digits added up to 12.
The tens digit was 3 bigger than the hundreds digit, and the units digit was 3 bigger than the tens digit.

What did I score?

1. Quadrantominoes

Liam has 4 quadrants of a circle, which has a diameter of 10cm.

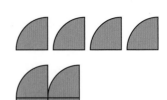

He uses all 4 quadrants to make this enclosed shape. Liam calls his enclosed shape a quadrantomino.

Explain to a friend why you think he decided on this name.

Make a copy of Liam's quadrantomino.

Explain to your friend how you did this.

The circumference of Liam's circle is approximately 31.4cm.

Work out the approximate perimeter of Liam's quadrantomino.

Explain to your friend how you did this.

> Investigate approximate perimeters of different quadrantominoes.

2. Robyn's Circles

Robyn draws a red circle with a diameter of 3cm.

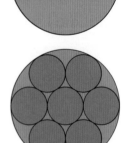

She finds that she can draw 7 identical green circles inside her red circle.

Copy Robyn's pattern of circles in her red circle.

Explain to a friend how you did this.

What is the diameter of each of the green circles?

Explain to your friend how you worked it out.

> Investigate doing what Robyn did with circles of different diameters.

1. Change these mixed numbers into fractions.

   a) $1\frac{4}{5} = \frac{}{5}$ b) $1\frac{8}{9} = \frac{}{9}$ c) $1\frac{3}{10} = \frac{}{10}$ d) $2\frac{1}{6} = \frac{}{6}$

   e) $2\frac{3}{4} = \frac{}{4}$ f) $2\frac{5}{8} = \frac{}{8}$ g) $3\frac{4}{7} = \frac{}{7}$ h) $4\frac{7}{12} = \frac{}{12}$

   i) $5\frac{3}{8} = \frac{}{8}$ j) $7\frac{2}{3} = \frac{}{3}$ k) $6\frac{1}{9} = \frac{}{9}$ l) $9\frac{5}{6} = \frac{}{6}$

2. Change these improper fractions to mixed numbers.

   a) $\frac{11}{3}$ b) $\frac{19}{4}$ c) $\frac{26}{9}$ d) $\frac{19}{2}$

   e) $\frac{27}{5}$ f) $\frac{37}{6}$ g) $\frac{49}{12}$ h) $\frac{35}{8}$

   i) $\frac{57}{10}$ j) $\frac{59}{11}$ k) $\frac{68}{7}$ l) $\frac{53}{9}$

3. Now fill in the missing numerators in your copy.

   a) $5 = \frac{}{3}$ b) $7 = \frac{}{6}$ c) $8 = \frac{}{9}$ d) $6 = \frac{}{8}$

   e) $\frac{}{5} = 9$ f) $\frac{}{11} = 6$ g) $\frac{}{4} = 12$ h) $\frac{}{12} = 8$

4. Add the following mixed numbers.

   a) $1\frac{2}{3} + 1\frac{1}{4}$ b) $2\frac{1}{5} + 1\frac{7}{10}$ c) $1\frac{5}{8} + 3\frac{2}{3}$

   d) $3\frac{5}{6} + 2\frac{3}{4}$ e) $4\frac{7}{9} + 2\frac{5}{6}$ f) $6\frac{4}{5} + 3\frac{3}{4}$

5. Find the difference between the following mixed numbers.

   a) $4\frac{3}{4} - 1\frac{1}{2}$ b) $5\frac{5}{6} - 1\frac{3}{4}$ c) $3\frac{8}{9} - 1\frac{1}{6}$

   d) $7\frac{7}{8} - 1\frac{2}{3}$ e) $6\frac{4}{5} - 3\frac{1}{3}$ f) $8\frac{5}{8} - 4\frac{1}{6}$

6. Find:

   a) $\frac{1}{4}$ of €376   b) $\frac{1}{7}$ of €336   c) $\frac{1}{9}$ of €423

   d) $\frac{1}{8}$ of €528   e) $\frac{1}{4}$ of €1972   f) $\frac{1}{6}$ of €2376

7. Find:

   a) $\frac{3}{7}$ of €945   b) $\frac{2}{5}$ of €695   c) $\frac{4}{9}$ of €2241

   d) $\frac{7}{8}$ of €2136   e) $\frac{5}{6}$ of €2304   f) $\frac{7}{12}$ of €2016

8. Work out the whole amount if:

a) $\frac{3}{4}$ = €1188

b) $\frac{4}{5}$ = €1032

c) $\frac{5}{7}$ = €2145

d) $\frac{7}{9}$ = €1022

e) $\frac{8}{11}$ = €2208

f) $\frac{9}{10}$ = €1431

9. What fraction is:

a) 50 mins of 1 hour

b) 60cm of 1 metre

c) €32 of €40

d) 750g of 1kg

e) 20 hours of 1 day

f) 21 days of September

Solve!

Flying High

A jumbo jet is carrying 350 passengers.

There are twice as many economy class passengers as business class passengers.

There are twice as many business class passengers as first class passengers.

How many of each class are on the plane?

Strategy hints!

1. Look for the important words in the question.
2. Have a go.
3. Think logically.

Extension

The total amount of money spent by all of the first class passengers for their seats equals the total amount of money spent by all of the economy class passengers for their seats.

How many times more expensive are the first class tickets than the economy class tickets?

1. Zoe's Improper Fractions

Zoe has 6 number cards.

| 1 | 2 | 3 | 4 | 5 | 6 |

She starts to make as many improper fractions as possible.

Each time, she uses 2 of her 6 number cards.

Here are 2 she makes.

Copy what Zoe did.

Is what she did correct?

Explain why to a friend.

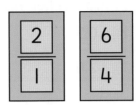

Make as many different improper fractions as you can for Zoe, using 2 of her number cards each time.

Explain to your friend how you did this.

Investigate sorting your fractions into those that are equivalent to whole numbers and those that are equivalent to mixed numbers.

2. Maili's Missing 4

Maili has 8 digit cards.

| 2 | 3 | 4 | 5 | 6 | 7 | 8 | 9 |

She tries to use 4 of her digits to complete this fraction statement correctly.

This is what she did.

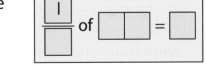

$\frac{1}{4}$ of $\boxed{2}\ \boxed{8}$ = $\boxed{7}$

Copy what Maili did.

Is what she did correct?

Explain why to a friend.

Investigate other ways of completing Maili's fraction statement correctly.

1. Change these fractions to decimal fractions.

    a) $\frac{1}{10}$ b) $\frac{8}{10}$ c) $\frac{5}{10}$ d) $\frac{4}{10}$

    e) $\frac{13}{10}$ f) $\frac{21}{10}$ g) $\frac{36}{10}$ h) $\frac{29}{10}$

2. Change these decimals to fractions.

    a) 0.5   b) 0.7   c) 0.2   d) 0.6

    e) 1.4   f) 2.6   g) 4.8   h) 7.1

3. Change these fractions to decimal fractions.

    a) $\frac{3}{100}$ b) $\frac{7}{100}$ c) $\frac{17}{100}$ d) $\frac{27}{100}$

    e) $\frac{16}{100}$ f) $\frac{35}{100}$ g) $\frac{56}{100}$ h) $\frac{80}{100}$

4. What is the value of the underlined digit in each of these numbers?

    a) 25.1$\underline{3}$ b) 1$\underline{7}$.42   c) 28.5$\underline{6}$

    d) $\underline{5}$1.8   e) 86.07   f) 39.4$\underline{5}$

5. Draw these numbers on notation boards.

    a) 18.06   b) 40.38   c) 6.47

    d) 93.5   e) 38.29   f) 80.05

6. Write these decimals as fractions.

    a) 0.009   b) 0.002   c) 0.019

    d) 0.048   e) 0.194   f) 0.703

7. What digit is in the thousandths place?

    a) 27.291   b) 45.025   c) 5.268

    d) 167.634   e) 0.296   f) 70.872

8. Round these decimals to the nearest whole number.
   a) 0.7
   b) 2.4
   c) 7.6
   d) 15.19
   e) 28.53
   f) 19.48
   g) 52.517
   h) 8.389
   i) 47.602

9. Put the following decimals in order, starting with the highest value.
   a) 3.78, 3.8, 3.87, 37.8
   b) 17.125, 17.215, 17.152, 17.251
   c) 46.3, 43.6, 43.58, 46.63
   d) 0.479, 0.497, 0.749, 0.794

10. a) $3.65 + 0.478 + 34.29$
    b) $75.095 + 713.8 + 2.57$
    c) $0.846 + 37.48 + 197.3$
    d) $537.284 + 7.17 + 29.65$
    e) $81.59 + 6.389 + 0.876$
    f) $9.146 + 74.38 + 196.28$

11. a) $3.15 - 2.7$
    b) $47.26 - 18.392$
    c) $175.3 - 69.78$
    d) $60.04 - 8.267$
    e) $5.4 - 2.81$
    f) $82.597 - 8.279$

12. a) 2.57×8
    b) 36.9×6
    c) 7.465×7
    d) 69.38×19
    e) 8.764×28
    f) 5.416×34

13. a) $0.465 \div 5$
    b) $12.64 \div 8$
    c) $338.4 \div 9$
    d) $91.8 \div 17$
    e) $72.8 \div 26$
    f) $140.6 \div 38$

Radio Waves

My favourite FM radio station is 101.8.

a) My mum listens to a radio station that is the same distance from 100.0 as my radio station, but is below 100. What radio station does Mum listen to?

b) My dad listens to a radio station that is halfway between my mum's radio station and 100.0. What radio station does Dad listen to?

Strategy hints!

1. Look for the important words in the question.

2. Use a drawing.

Extension

My sister has a favourite radio station. When rounded to the nearest whole number, it equals 105. It has more odd digits than even digits. One of the digits is zero. It would be shown by 16 light bars on a calculator. It has 1 decimal place.

What radio station does my sister listen to?

1. A Decimal Cross

Claire has 6 decimal number cards.

| 0.1 | 0.2 | 0.3 | 0.4 | 0.5 | 0.6 |

She places the 6 decimal number cards
in this cross so that the sum of the 3
numbers in the row equals the sum of
the 4 numbers in the column.

Copy what Claire did.

Is what she did correct?

Explain why.

		0.1	
0.5	0.4	0.2
		0.6
		0.3

> Investigate different ways of making the sums of the
> numbers in the row and the column equal.

2. More Than Decimals

Mark has 4 digit cards.

| 1 | 2 | 3 | 4 |

He wants to use his 4 digit cards to make this decimal 'more than'
statement true.

0 • [ ][ ] > 0 • [ ][ ]

This is what he did.   0 • 2 1 > 0 • 4 3

Copy what Mark did.

Is what Mark did correct?

Explain why.

> Investigate different ways of
> completing the decimal
> 'more than' statement.

1. The table lists the cost of purchasing 4 of the listed items. Work out how much it would have cost to buy 9 of each of these items. Write the answer in your copy.

Product	4 items	9 items
Bananas	€1.92	
Tins of chopped tomatoes	€2.36	
Litres of milk	€3.88	
Box of chocolates	€9.44	
Cucumbers	€2.76	
Mugs	€5.52	

2. Work out the weekly wages of the following people. Write the answer in your copy.

Name	Hourly Pay	Hours Worked per Day	Days Worked per Week	Weekly Wage
Wendy	€9.50	6	3	
Oliver	€8.80	9	5	
Raymond	€12	7	6	
Kevin	€10.20	5	4	
Ernie	€13.60	8	5	
Rachael	€14	9	7	

3. Copy this table in your copybook, then fill in the blanks.

Name	Hourly Pay	Hours Worked per Day	Days Worked per Week	Weekly Wage
Colin		7	5	€385
Angela	€9.50		6	€342
Susan	€13	5		€260
Helen		8	6	€600

4. My true love went shopping again and this time she bought 6 geese @ €49 each and 7 swans @ €57 each. How much did she spend in total? How much change did she have out of €900?

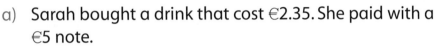

Solve!   19. Money

Change Up

a) Sarah bought a drink that cost €2.35. She paid with a €5 note.

She received her change in the fewest possible coins. Which coins did Sarah receive?

b) Sarah put the change in her purse. She noticed that she now had 7 coins worth €3.90.

What coins were already in Sarah's purse before she received her change?

Strategy hints!

1. Look for the important words in the question.
2. Have a go.
3. Use a drawing.

Extension

a) Sarah paid €10 for a drink and sandwich, which cost €5.35. She received her change in the fewest possible coins. Which coins was Sarah given?

b) When Sarah put the change in her purse, she noticed that she now had 10 coins, 5 of them the same, worth €5.10. What coins were in Sarah's purse before receiving her change?

1. A Book of 10 Stamps

Stephen buys a book of 10 postage stamps.

The book contains a mixture of 55c and 75c stamps.

Stephen says, 'I think that the book of 10 stamps will cost me €6.30.'

Could what Stephen said be correct?

Explain why to a friend.

Investigate other possible costs for the book of 10 stamps.

2. Pizza Delight

Lisa sells 4 sizes of pizza at Pizza Delight Takeaway.

| 8cm | 10cm | 12cm | 14cm |
| €2.00 | €3.20 | €4.40 | €5.60 |

Lisa decides that it is time the shop sold a 16cm pizza.

Her chef says, 'Based on the sizes and prices of the other 4 pizzas we make, I think a 16cm pizza should sell for €6.00.'

Explain to a friend how you think the chef worked out this price.

Investigate possible prices of larger and smaller pizzas using the same way of pricing the other pizzas.

1. Try these. See if they have more than 1 possible answer. If they have more than 1 possible answer, work out each of the possibilities.

   a) $4 + 7 + 8$

   b) $8 + 15 - 6$

   c) $16 - 7 + 5$

   d) $28 - 8 - 9$

   e) $8 \times 3 + 4$

   f) $5 + 7 \times 8$

   g) $3 \times 6 - 6$

   h) $14 - 6 \times 2$

   i) $2 \times 4 \times 7$

   j) $28 \div 4 + 3$

   k) $27 + 9 \div 3$

   l) $48 - 8 \div 8$

2. Now try these.

   a) $(64 + 47) - 38$

   b) $68 + (53 - 29)$

   c) $83 - (36 + 27)$

   d) $6 \times (27 + 15)$

   e) $(29 + 18) \times 8$

   f) $58 + (9 \times 7)$

   g) $73 - (8 \times 7)$

   h) $(84 - 39) - 26$

   i) $91 - (82 - 58)$

   j) $(127 - 55) \div 9$

   k) $56 - (84 \div 12)$

   l) $108 \div (53 - 44)$

3. Use your calculator to work these out.

   a) $(18 \times 69) + 2095$

   b) $(1674 + 1836) - 1967$

   c) $(912 \div 24) \times 68$

   d) $(47 \times 56) \div 7$

   e) $3043 - (752 \div 8)$

   f) $(3267 + 856) \div 7$

4. Can you spot the pattern?

   a) 5, 10, 20, 35, 55, 80, 110

   b) 84, 72, 61, 51, 42, 34

   c) 2, 6, 18, 54, 162, 486

   d) 18, 24, 21, 27, 24, 30

   e) 144, 72, 36, 18, 9

   f) 1, 3, 6, 10, 15, 21

5. Work out the patterns and fill in the missing terms.

    a) 7, 14, 21, 28, ____, ____, ____

    b) 121, 110, 99, 88, ____, ____, ____

    c) 2, 3, 5, 8, 12, ____, ____, ____

    d) 75, 60, 70, 55, 65, ____, ____, ____

    e) 4, 6, 10, 16, 24, ____, ____, ____

    f) 79, 66, 55, 46, 39, ____, ____, ____

Solve!

20. Rules and Properties

Signs in Place

a) Use the numbers 7, 2 and 5 in that order along with +, −, × or ÷ signs to create a sum that equals 9.

b) Use the numbers 24, 6 and 5 in that order along with +, −, × or ÷ signs to create a sum that equals 20.

Extension

a) Use the numbers 7, 2 and 5 in that order along with +, −, × or ÷ signs to create a sum that equals 25.

b) Use the numbers 32, 2, 4 and 5 in that order along with +, −, × or ÷ signs to create a sum that equals 21.

Strategy hints!

1. Look for the important words in the question.

2. Have a go.

3. Think logically.

1. Four of the Same

Julie has 4 operations cards and a blank calculation.

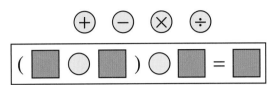

Julie chooses a pair of operations cards and the number 2 for each box in the calculation to make the statement correct.

This is what she did.

Copy what Julie did.

Is what she did correct?

Explain why to a friend.

> Investigate ways of choosing pairs of operations and the same number for each box to make the statement correct.

2. What Are the Differences?

Karen starts to make the multiply by 2 sequence.

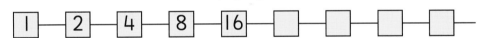

Copy, complete and extend Karen's sequence.

Karen works out differences of next-to numbers in the sequence and keeps repeating this to make difference sequences.

Copy, complete and extend what Karen did.

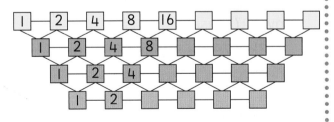

Is what Karen did correct?

Explain why to a friend.

Describe patterns in the sequences to your friend.

> Investigate multiplying by 3, 4, 5, etc. sequences.

1. Write your answer in your copy.

   a) 1m 26cm = _____ cm
   b) 308cm = __m ____ cm
   c) 2m 69cm = _____ m
   d) 4m 7cm = _____ m
   e) 7018m = __km _____ m
   f) 6km 184m = _____ m
   g) 5.47km = _____ m
   h) 726m = _____ km

2. Now try these. You can choose whichever way you prefer, but it's very important that you record the unit of measurement in your answer.

   a) 4m 36cm + 274cm + 3.98m
   b) 85cm + 2m 9cm + 6.49m
   c) 7.03m + 408cm + $2\frac{3}{4}$m
   d) 7m 16cm + 4.27m + 8cm
   e) $3\frac{4}{5}$m + 576cm + 2.68m
   f) 5.87m + 2m 38cm + 913cm

3. Now try these. You have the same choices with subtraction.

   a) 6m 13cm – 276cm
   b) 4.04m – 3m 49cm
   c) 527cm – 2.6m
   d) 7m 31cm – 5.56m
   e) 9m 42cm – 363cm
   f) $8\frac{7}{10}$m – 6m 83cm

4. Now try these.

   a) 3km 79m + 486m + 5.19km
   b) $2\frac{178}{1000}$ km + 3km 365m + 4093m
   c) 7.41km + $3\frac{3}{5}$km + 4km 287m
   d) 6km 9m + 2.95km + 780m
   e) 6km 153m – 4.378km
   f) 8264m – 3km 39m
   g) 7.03km – 795m
   h) $7\frac{1}{4}$km – 6km 684m

5. Write the answer in your copy.

a) 14mm = ___cm ___mm

b) 2cm 7mm = ____cm

c) 4.3cm = ____mm

d) 3cm 8mm = ____mm

e) 106mm = ___cm ___mm

f) ____cm = 12cm 9mm

6. Now try these.

a) 7cm 3mm + 57mm + 3.6cm

b) 76mm + $5\frac{3}{5}$cm + 3cm 8mm

c) 126mm + 7.3cm + $9\frac{3}{10}$cm

d) 24mm + 6cm 7mm + 9.6cm

e) 7cm 2mm – 56mm

f) 132mm – 8.4cm

g) 15.2cm – 6cm 7mm

h) 12cm 7mm – 109mm

7. Choose whichever way you prefer and work out the answers to these. Remember to record the unit of measurement in your answer.

a) 3m 28cm × 9

b) 347cm × 6

c) 5.74m × 8

d) 6km 59m × 7

e) 4.364km × 12

f) 7189m × 5

8. Now try these.

a) 345mm ÷ 5

b) 2km 334m ÷ 6

c) 39.69m ÷ 7

d) 61m 12cm ÷ 8

e) 78.3cm ÷ 9

f) 6912m ÷ 12

9. Now work out the perimeters of these rectangles.

a) length 34cm
   width 26cm

b) length 47mm
   width 38mm

c) length 65m
   width 53m

d) length 9.6cm
   width 5.9cm

e) length 1.45m
   width 0.76m

f) length 3.135km
   width 2.097km

Paddock Puzzle

Farmer Stan has a paddock in which he keeps his favourite bull, Malcolm.

Malcolm's paddock has a fence around it that is 500 metres in perimeter.

The length of the paddock is 200 metres.

a) What is the width of the paddock?

b) In the middle of each side of the fence is a gate. What is the shortest distance between any 2 gates?

Strategy hints!

1. Look for the important words in the question.
2. Use a drawing.
3. Make a model.

Extension

Farmer Stan's favourite pig is called Tinkerbell.

Tinkerbell lives in a square pen that has a perimeter of 34 metres. How long is each side of Tinkerbell's pen?

1. Classroom to Hall

Two children in 5th Class estimate the distance from their classroom to the school hall.

These were their estimates.

They each measured the distance.
Aimee made an error of 5 metres.
Sam made an error of 10 metres.
What was the actual distance from their classroom to the school hall?
Explain to a friend how you decided.

Aimee	Sam
115m	130m

> Investigate estimating and then measuring the distance from every classroom to the hall in your school.

2. Paper Sizes

Siobhán finds that in most countries, sheets of paper come in standard sizes, which are given the names A0 to A10.

The sheet A0 has a height of 1189mm and a width of 841mm.

Make a sheet the same size as an A0.

Explain to a friend how you did this.

What is the ratio of height to width of A0 paper?

Explain to your friend how you worked it out.

What is the area of a sheet of A0 paper?

Explain to your friend how you worked it out.

A0

1189mm

841mm

> Investigate the area and the ratio of height to width of A1, A2, A3, etc. sheets of paper.

1. Identify the following 3-D shapes from the list below.

cube   sphere   cuboid   cylinder   cone   pyramid

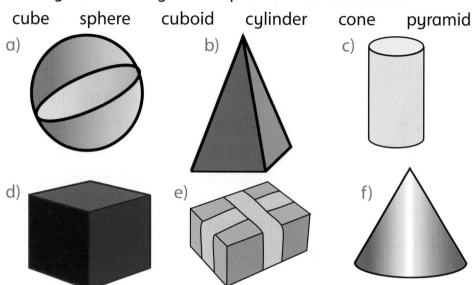

a)   b)   c)

d)   e)   f)

2. Name the following 3-D shapes from their nets.

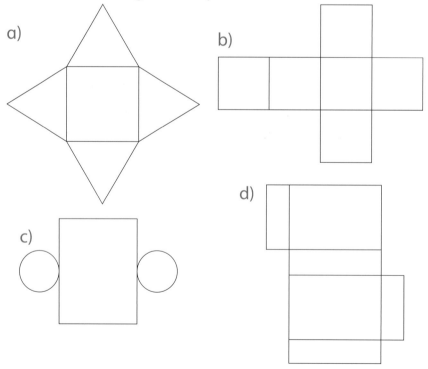

a)

b)

c)

d)

3. Choose 1 of the nets and construct the 3-D shape.

4. Draw and fill in the following table in your copy.

Shape	Number of Faces	Number of Edges	Number of Vertices (Corners)
Cuboid			
Pyramid			
Cube			
Cylinder			
Tetrahedron			
Triangular prism			

Solve!   22. 3-D Shapes

Build a Cube

Alana sticks together 2 cubes and makes a rectangular prism.

a) To turn this rectangular prism into a cube, how many more cubes must Alana add?

b) When her cube is finished, Alana counts the number of edges, faces and vertices (corners) on the 3-D object she has made. How many of each does she count?

Strategy hints!

1. Look for the important words in the question.
2. Use a drawing.
3. Make a model.

Extension

Alana sticks together 12 cubes and makes a tower that is 6 cubes high.

a) How many faces of the small cubes can be seen on the new object?

b) How many edges does the new object have overall?

c) How many vertices does the new object have overall?

1. Brendan's Cuboids

Brendan has lots of these cubes.

Here are 2 cuboids, A and B, which
Brendan makes using his cubes.

Use your own cubes to make each cuboid.

How many cubes did you need to make each cuboid?

Explain to a friend how you did this.

Copy and complete this table for Brendan.

	Length	Height	Depth	Number of Cubes
Cuboid A				
Cuboid B				

Explain to your friend what the table is
about and how you completed it.

Investigate making
different cuboids.

2. Eimear's Hexominoes

Eimear uses 6 squares to make this polygon.

Draw Eimear's polygon.

Explain to a friend how you did this.

Eimear says, 'My polygon is called an
hexomino because it is made of 6 squares
put side to side.'

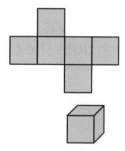

She claims that when the hexomino is folded
along the joined sides, it makes a
cube.

Is what Eimear claims true?

Explain why to your friend.

Investigate making other
hexominoes that fold to
make cubes.

1. Express these fractions as percentages.

   a) $\dfrac{7}{100}$ b) $\dfrac{15}{100}$ c) $\dfrac{89}{100}$

   d) $\dfrac{56}{100}$ e) $\dfrac{8}{100}$ f) $\dfrac{67}{100}$

   g) $\dfrac{94}{100}$ h) $\dfrac{39}{100}$ i) $\dfrac{72}{100}$

2. Express these percentages as fractions.

   a) $23\% = \dfrac{}{100}$ b) 16%   c) 5%

   d) 31%   e) 76%   f) 42%

   g) 54%   h) 83%   i) 97%

3. Convert these decimals to fractions and then percentages.

   a) $0.13 = \dfrac{}{100} = \underline{\quad}\%$ b) 0.58   c) 0.27

   d) 0.39   e) 0.71   f) 0.06

   g) 0.94   h) 0.65   i) 0.82

4. Find:

   a) 50% of €146   b) 10% of €7.90   c) 25% of €3.84

   d) 75% of €312   e) 20% of €875   f) 40% of €790

5. Now try these.

   a) 30% of 180   b) 70% of 430   c) 80% of 675

   d) 15% of 640   e) 45% of 940   f) 85% of 720

6. Now try these using your calculator.

   a) 24% of 1700   b) 73% of 3420   c) 9% of 5210

   d) 59% of 6400   e) 67% of 2780   f) 81% of 4170

7. Complete this table in your copy to show the sale prices.

Item	Old Price	% Discount	Sale Price
Coat	€105	40%	
Shoes	€90	10%	
Freezer	€392	25%	
Jacket	€48	75%	
TV	€270	30%	
Dishwasher	€420	35%	

8. Complete this table in your copy to show the increased prices.

Item	Old Price	% Increase	New Price
CD	€10.60	50%	
Roller blades	€80	20%	
Hoodie	€29.60	25%	
Bed	€460	15%	
Mobile phone	€95	40%	
Tablet PC	€220	35%	

Solve!   23. Percentages

Many Times Bigger

I am a 4-digit number.

I contain the digits 3, 7, 9 and 9.

The value of 1 of my digits is 100 times bigger than the value of 1 of my other digits.

Find all the numbers that I can be.

Extension

If 2 of the same digits are 3 places apart in a number, how many times bigger in value is 1 digit than the other?

Strategy hints!

1. Look for the important words in the question.

2. Think logically.

1. Percentage Calculations

Kate has 10 digit cards and a missing digits percentage calculation.

0	1	2	3	4
5	6	7	8	9

Kate chooses 5 of her 10 digit cards to complete the percentage calculation.

☐ ☐ % of ☐ 0 = ☐ ☐

Copy what Kate did.

2 5 % of 4 0 = 1 0

Is what she did correct?

Explain why to a friend.

> Investigate other ways of completing the percentage calculation correctly.

2. Buying and Selling

Nicola bought a chair at an auction.

She sold the chair for a 10% profit.

The amount of profit Nicola made was a whole number of euros and less than €100.

Eve says, 'I think Nicola bought the chair for €50 and made a profit of €5.'

Could what Eve said be correct?

Explain to a friend how you decided.

> Investigate how much the chair could have cost, the profit and the selling price.

1. This table shows the maximum and minimum
    temperatures recorded in various cities during
    the course of a day. Work out the difference in
    temperature between the maximum and
    minimum values for each city.

City	Minimum Temperature	Maximum Temperature
Belfast	−3°C	7°C
Dublin	−1°C	12°C
Edinburgh	−6°C	11°C
Glasgow	−4°C	7°C
London	−8°C	4°C
Manchester	−5°C	8°C

2. Aisling had €26 in her bank account. She used her debit card to
    buy a pair of sandals for €14.99 and a pair of jeans for €29.99.
    What is her new bank balance?

3. The following people work in a building with
    12 floors and an underground car park with 4
    different levels. They each work on different
    floors and use the lift to get from there to the
    car park and back. Draw this table in your
    copy and fill in the gaps.

	Floor Entered Lift	Floors Travelled	Floor Exited Lift
Carmel	7	9 down	
Noel	−3		11
Katherine		6 down	−4
Tony	−2	11 up	
Miriam	12		−1
Brian		3 up	1

4. The tip of an iceberg is measured as 23m above sea level, whereas the base of the iceberg is −79m below sea level. What is the total height of the iceberg?

Solve!   25. Directed Numbers

Going Up

Albert enters a lift at the ground floor of a building.

He goes up 7 levels, then down 5 levels, then up 9 levels and then down 4 levels.

a) What level is Albert on now?

b) Albert did not visit the top 2 levels of the building. Including the ground floor, how many levels are in the building?

Strategy hints!

1. Look for the important words in the question.

2. Use a drawing.

Extension

Albert enters a building where the lift is broken. He has to walk to the top level. After walking to the 4th level, he discovers that he is not even half of the way to the top.

What is the smallest number of levels that the building could have?

1. Cloud Covering

Katie makes a count on sequence with some numbers hidden by a cloud.

It starts with the directed number −11 and ends with the directed number +13.

Only the numbers −11 and +13 are not covered by the cloud.

Ciarán says, 'I predict that there is only 1 directed number under the cloud and that number is +1.'

Could what Ciarán said be correct?

Explain why to a friend.

> Investigate which directed numbers could be hidden under the cloud.

2. Freezing Cold

Donal lives in a very cold town.

Over a period of 4 days the temperature dropped the same number of whole degrees each day until at the start of day 4 it was −27°C.

| Start of day 1 | Start of day 2 | Start of day 3 | Start of day 4 |
| ?°C | ?°C | ?°C | -27°C |

Donal says, 'At the start of day 1 the temperature was greater than 0°C.'

Michael says, 'I think the temperature at the start of day 1 was +3°C.'

Could what Micheal said be true?

Explain why to a friend.

If Micheal was correct, what were the temperatures at the start of days 2 and 3?

Explain to your friend how you worked this out.

> Investigate what other temperatures there could have been at the start of days 1, 2 and 3.

1. Write these as grams.
   - a) 6 kilograms
   - b) $5\frac{1}{4}$ kilograms
   - c) $2\frac{4}{5}$ kilograms
   - d) $\frac{9}{1000}$ kilogram
   - e) $\frac{724}{1000}$ kilogram
   - f) $5\frac{83}{1000}$ kilograms

2. Write these as i) kg and g, and ii) kg.
   - a) 2871g
   - b) 7804g
   - c) 496g
   - d) 8378g
   - e) 39g
   - f) 4230g

3. Work out the answers to these.
   - a) 5.37kg + 1980g + 3kg 528g
   - b) 5287g + 7kg 178g + 2.9kg
   - c) 3kg 587g + 1.027kg + 6370g
   - d) 4.8kg + 3680g + 4kg 29g

4. Now try these.
   - a) 7kg 324g – 857g
   - b) 5.03kg – 2kg 86g
   - c) 5108g – 2.64kg
   - d) 7kg 46g – 4.283kg

5. And these.
   - a) 7kg 184g × 6
   - b) 4098g × 9
   - c) 3.472kg × 7
   - d) 3450g × 17
   - e) 6.95kg × 28
   - f) 2kg 79g × 34

6. Finally, try these.
   - a) 2688g ÷ 7
   - b) 3kg 933g ÷ 9
   - c) 2.31kg ÷ 7
   - d) 0.826kg ÷ 14
   - e) 0.448kg ÷ 16
   - f) 1kg 92g ÷ 28

7. A furniture removals team was carrying a wardrobe down a flight of stairs. The wardrobe weighed 83kg 24g. Unfortunately, the team dropped the wardrobe down the stairs, resulting in both doors falling off the wardrobe. The wardrobe now weighed 59.67kg. How heavy were the doors?

8. A troupe of acrobats in a circus finished their act with 1 member of the troupe, Andre, supporting all of the other 3 members of the team. Sasha weighs 68kg 168g, Yuri weighs 87.92kg and Natalya weighs 71 $\frac{3}{4}$ kg. How much weight was Andre supporting in total?

9. A school bought 16 laptops for its laptop trolley. If 1 laptop weighs 3kg 58g, how much would the 16 laptops weigh in total?

10. A box of 24 mugs weighs 2kg 508g. If the box weighs 852g, how much does each mug weigh?

Solve!   26. Weight

Heavy Water

1 litre of water weighs 1 kilogram.

A glass weighs 200 grams.

Barnaby pours out 100 millilitres of water, drinks half, then puts down the glass.

When he picks it up again, what total weight is he picking up?

Strategy hints!

1. Look for the important words in the question.

2. Think logically.

Extension

Uncle Brendan gets out of the shower and weighs himself.

The scales show 99kg.

He drinks a litre of water and then puts on his shorts and T-shirt.

The shorts and T-shirt weigh 500g altogether.

Uncle Brendan than gets onto the scales again.

What is his weight now?

1. Decimal Kilograms

Isobel has 2 sets of 5 digit cards and a missing digits grams to kilograms statement.

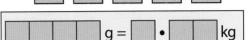

Isobel uses 7 of her digit cards to complete the statement.

This is what she did.

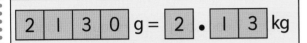

$$\boxed{2}\ \boxed{1}\ \boxed{3}\ \boxed{0}\ g = \boxed{2} \bullet \boxed{1}\ \boxed{3}\ kg$$

Copy what Isobel did.

Is what she did correct?

Explain why to a friend.

> Investigate ways to complete Isobel's statement correctly.

2. Weighing Euro Coins

Diarmuid has 3 coins, a 1c, a 20c and a €2, and a balance.

He feels each of the coins and decides that the €2 coin is the heaviest and the 1c coin is the lightest.

Do you think what Diarmuid decides is correct?

What makes you think this?

Diarmuid says, 'Four 1c coins balance one €2 coin.' Is what Diarmuid said correct?

Explain to a friend how you decided.

> Investigate ways of weighing each type of euro coin.

1. Construct a bar chart showing the favourite snack of those surveyed, represented in the table below.

Crackers	Fruit	Crisps	Yoghurt	Carrot Sticks
10	22	14	18	16

2. Record the maximum and minimum temperatures of the 5 days on a multiple bar chart.

	Monday	Tuesday	Wednesday	Thursday	Friday
Maximum	19	17	13	16	18
Minimum	11	12	8	10	13

3. This pie chart shows the favourite pizza topping of 240 children. Can you work out from the pie chart how many children preferred each individual topping?

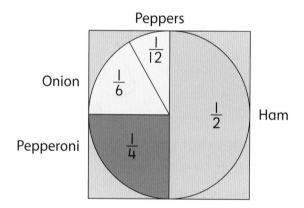

4. Construct a pie chart to represent what season each group of people's birthdays falls in.

Season	Spring	Summer	Autumn	Winter
Number of People	18	3	6	9

Favourite Pastimes

40 teachers were surveyed about their favourite pastimes.

$\frac{1}{2}$ voted for hiking and the other $\frac{1}{2}$ voted for listening to music.

One out of 8 voted for reading.

There were 4 times the votes for watching movies as for gardening.

a) How many teachers voted for gardening?

b) Make a chart or graph of the votes.

> **Strategy hints!**
> 1. Look for the important words in the question.
> 2. Use a table or a chart.

Extension

36 students were surveyed about their favourite pastimes.

One out of 3 voted for TV. Sport came in second.

One out of 4 voted for computer games.

The difference between computer games and visiting friends was 4.

a) How many votes did each pastime get?

b) Make a chart or graph of the votes.

1. First Names

Here are 6 children in the 5th Class at St Joseph's Primary School.

Who has the fewest letters in their first name?

Seán   Amy   Ciarán   Aron   Emma   Ailis

Explain how you worked it out to a friend.

Sean draws a pictogram of the number of letters in the first names of the 6 children.

Copy Sean's pictogram.

3 letters	😊		
4 letters	😊	😊	😊
5 letters	😊		
6 letters	😊		

Explain what the pictogram tells you about the frequency of the number of letters in the 6 first names.

> Investigate drawing charts of the number of letters in the first names of children in your class.

2. Three Coins

Anna has three 10c coins.

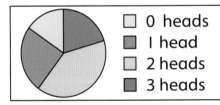

She tosses the 3 coins 20 times, each time recording the number of heads showing.

Anna draws a pie chart of her results.

Copy Anna's pie chart.

Estimate the number of times 0 heads, 1 head, 2 heads and 3 heads occurred out of the 20 tosses.

Explain to a friend how you worked this out.

☐ 0 heads
■ 1 head
☐ 2 heads
■ 3 heads

> Investigate doing what Anna did 3 times and compare results.

1. State whether the area of the following objects would be measured in cm² or m².

   a) piece of art paper   b) school yard

   c) football pitch   d) DVD cover

   e) birthday card   f) basketball backboard

2. Jenny was experimenting with using different sizes of paper for painting a picture of her puppy. Work out the area of each different size of paper from the dimensions given.

   a) length 19cm
      width 13cm

   b) length 27cm
      width 24cm

   c) length 38cm
      width 26cm

   d) length 37cm
      width 23cm

   e) length 45cm
      width 35cm

   f) length 47cm
      width 36cm

3. Draw the following rectangles into your copy. Decorate them and calculate their area.

   a) **Rectangle 1**
      length 9cm
      width 4cm

   b) **Rectangle 2**
      length 8cm
      width 6cm

   c) **Rectangle 3**
      length 7cm
      width 3cm

   d) **Rectangle 4**
      length 8cm
      width 5cm

   e) **Rectangle 5**
      length 10cm
      width 7cm

   f) **Rectangle 6**
      length 12cm
      width 9cm

4. Sam was cutting the grass in his back garden. If the garden is 9.8m long and 13m wide, what is the area of the garden?

5. Mike's TV screen is 68cm wide and 36cm long. Joe's TV screen is 57cm wide and 43cm long. Whose TV screen has the greater area?

Solve!   28. Area 1

Tiling Times

Tina the tiler is using square tiles that measure 10 centimetres on each side.

Tina needs to cover an area that is $\frac{1}{2}$ metre wide and 1 metre long.

How many tiles does Tina need to complete the job?

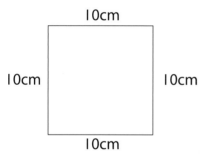

10cm

10cm   10cm

10cm

Strategy hints!
1. Look for the important words in the question.
2. Use a drawing.
3. Make a model.

Extension

The job looks so good when it is finished that Tina decides to tile another area.

She makes the new area twice as wide and 3 times as long.

How many times longer will this new job take Tina to finish compared with the first job?

1. Equal Areas

Reece has lots of 3×3 square grids.

He draws polygons on 3 of his grids.

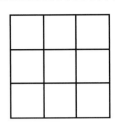

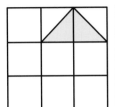 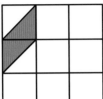 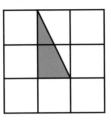

Copy and colour the 3 polygons.

Explain the special names and properties of each polygon to a friend.

Reece says, 'Each of my polygons has an area equal to 1 square.'
Is what Reece said correct?

Explain how you worked them out to your friend.

> Investigate drawing polygons, each having an area of 1, 2, 3, 4, etc. squares.

2. Covering an Island

Michaela draws an island.

She covers her island with 10mm squares.

Michaela estimates that in total, 7 squares cover the island.

What is Michaela's estimate in square centimetres?

Explain to a friend how you decided.

Is Michaela's estimate a good one?

Explain why to a friend.

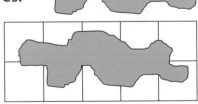

> Investigate covering Michaela's island with different-sized squares.

1. Can you write these as litres and millilitres?

    a) 3276ml   b) 1.493l   c) 3040ml

    d) 2.18l   e) 8253ml   f) 6.7l

    g) 9018ml   h) 5.265l   i) 48ml

2. Can you write these capacities as millilitres?

    a) 1 litre 248ml   b) 4 litres 6ml   c) 2 litres 170ml

    d) 5 litres 2ml   e) 3.725l   f) 7.36l

    g) 5.9l   h) 0.064l   i) 8.059l

3. Can you write these capacities as litres using the decimal point?

    a) 1 litre 485ml   b) 3870ml   c) 2 litres 9ml

    d) 6 litres 38ml   e) 549ml   f) 3ml

4. Now try these. Remember to change them to the same units before you start.

    a) 2l 19ml + 1.56l + 397ml   b) 1045ml + 6l 204ml + 2.74l

    c) 5.147l + 3270ml + 2l 632ml   d) 3.8l + 76ml + 2l 5ml

    e) 4027ml + 1l 560ml + 7.49l   f) 3l 78ml + 0.358l + 6923ml

5. a) 4l 61ml – 2.85 litres   b) 3005ml – 1.79l

   c) 7.264 litres – 3l 467ml   d) 9l 35ml – 6749ml

   e) 7107ml – 3.536 litres   f) 11.3 litres – 7l 423ml

6. Have a go at these.

   a) 3256ml × 7

   b) 1.937l × 9

   c) 5l 34ml × 8

   d) 2.416l × 13

   e) 3l 527ml × 26

   f) 4813ml × 34

7. Now try these.

   a) 2304ml ÷ 6

   b) 2l 536ml ÷ 8

   c) 4.37l ÷ 5

   d) 40.5l ÷ 15

   e) 901ml ÷ 17

   f) 1l 288ml ÷ 23

8. If there are 195ml in a carton of orange juice, how much juice would there be in 28 such cartons?

9. Ted filled the empty petrol tank of his car with 28l 413ml. After driving for a couple of days, there were 15.845l left in the tank. How much petrol had Ted used?

10. Martina had only 79ml of water left in her bottle. She topped it up with 0.638l from the tap. How much water was now in her bottle?

11. From a water cooler containing 10.14l, 39 cups of water were filled to the top, leaving the cooler empty. What was the capacity of each cup?

Bucket Brigade

Ryan has 3 empty buckets.

Bucket A can hold 10 litres, bucket B can hold 5 litres and bucket C can hold 3 litres.

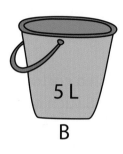

10 L

A

5 L

B

3 L

C

He fills up bucket A.

He now needs to make sure that the 2 other buckets hold exactly 3 litres each.

How can he make sure that there is exactly 3 litres in each of the 2 buckets?

Strategy hints!

1. Look for the important words in the question.
2. Have a go.
3. Use a table or a chart.

Extension

Ryan then tips all of the water back into bucket A.

He now wants to make sure that bucket A holds exactly 8 litres of water.

How can he do this?

1. Aoife's Statement

Aoife has 2 sets of digit cards and a missing digits capacity statement.

0	1	2	4	5	7	8
0	1	2	4	5	7	8

This is how Aoife completed the statement.

$\frac{1}{4}$ litre = | 2 | 5 | 0 | ml

$\frac{\square}{\square}$ litre = | | | | ml

Copy what Aoife did.

Is what Aoife did correct?

Explain how you decided to a friend.

Investigate other ways Aoife could have completed the capacity statement.

2. Daragh's Spoons

Daragh has 5 different spoons.

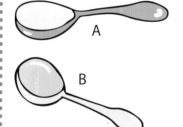

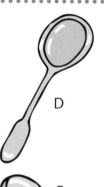

A
B
C
D
E

Inspect the pictures of Daragh's 5 spoons.

Estimate the order of how much each holds.

Explain to a friend how you decided.

Daragh says, 'Spoon A holds 10 millilitres of water.'
Could what Daragh said be correct?

Explain how you decided to your friend.

Investigate measuring how many millilitres of water different spoons hold.

1. Find the average of each of these number sets. Estimate your answer first.

   a) 6.9, 6.5, 7.7, 7.3, 6.1   b) 152ml 134ml, 146ml

   c) €3.12, €2.95, €1.73, €4.08   d) 175g, 295g, 349g

   e) 1009, 998, 1005, 992   f) 2.389km, 1.927km, 2.309km

2. The following shows the heights of 5 friends.

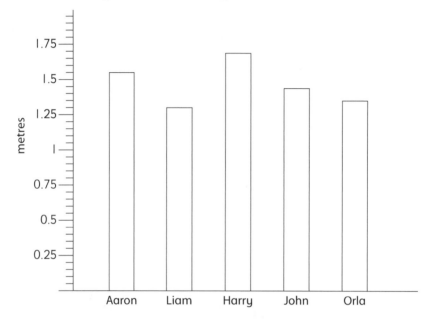

   a) What is the average height of the friends?

   b) How many of the friends are above the average and below the average?

   c) What is the average height of the boys?

   d) If a 6th friend, Jess, joined the group of friends and she was 1.29m tall, how would that change the average height in the group?

   e) What would be the average height of the girls?

3.

Song	Number of Downloads
Song for My Pony	32
Cry Me an Ocean	1874
Singing in the Snow	985
Heartache Hostel	3481

a) What was the average number of downloads of the 4 songs?

b) If a 5th song, 'That's What Makes You Quite Nice', was downloaded 2193 times, how would that change the average?

Solve!   30. Averages

Champion Surfer

Dave is a champion surfer.

His 6 winning rides at Bells Beach are scored out of 10.

Ride	1	2	3	4	5	6	Total
Score	?	10	10	?	10	?	

Two of Dave's missing rides scored the same number of points.

What is the lowest score Dave could have been given for any ride?

Strategy hints!

1. Look for the important words in the question.

2. Use a table or a chart.

Extension

Ben came 2nd in the championships. He had 2 rides that were better than Dave's rides, but he lost to him by 2 points.

What is the maximum number of perfect 10s that Ben could have scored?

1. The Average Is 4

Lorcan has 9 digit cards and a set of 4 blank cards.

Lorcan says, 'I am going to use 4 of my 1 to 9 digit cards for the 4 blank cards. The average of the 4 digit cards I choose is 4.'

| 1 | 2 | 3 | 4 | 5 | 6 | 7 | 8 | 9 |

| | | | |

This is what Lorcan did.

| 5 | 2 | 1 | 7 |

Make a copy of what Lorcan did.

Is what Lorcan did correct?

Explain why to a friend.

Investigate other sets of 4 digit cards that Lorcan could have chosen.

2. Class Heights

Work with 2 friends.

Measure the height of every child in your class.

Make a record of what you do and your findings.

Calculate the average height of the boys in your class.

Explain to a friend how you did this.

Calculate the average height of the girls in your class.

Explain to your friend how you did this.

Calculate the average height of the children in your class.

Explain to your friend how you did this.

Investigate choosing pairs to make the average heights of each pair and the class nearly the same.

1. Estimate and measure the areas of these rectangles.

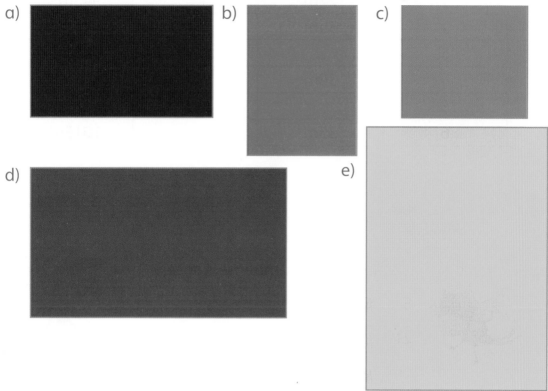

a)

b)

c)

d)

e)

2. Estimate and measure the areas of the following shapes.

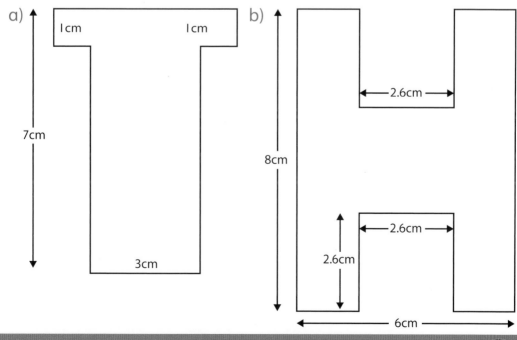

a) 1cm   1cm   7cm   3cm

b) 2.6cm   8cm   2.6cm   2.6cm   6cm

3. Fill in the missing measurements of these car parks in your copy.

Car Park	Length	Width	Area
1	27m		945m²
2	34m	28m	
3		26m	676m²
4	39m	23m	
5		33m	891m²
6	35m		1015m²

Solve! 31. Area 2

Symbol Shake-up

Lily sees these number sentences.

8 # 4 = 2

21 # 13 = 9

10 # 7 = 3

What is the answer to the following?

a) 16 # 4 =

b) 100 # 8 =

Strategy hints!

1. Look for the important words in the question.

2. Look for a pattern.

3. Think logically.

Extension

Lily sees these number sentences.

9 * 4 = 5

15 * 8 = 7

18 * 10 = 8

What is the answer to the following?

a) 36 * 6 =

b) 45 * 3 =

1. Shane's Sticks

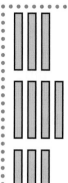

Shane has 10 sticks.

Each stick is 5cm long.

He uses all 10 sticks to make this polygon.

Make a copy of Shane's polygon.

How many degrees is in each internal angle?

Explain to a friend how you worked them out.

Shane says, 'My 6-sided polygon has a perimeter of 50cm and an area of 125cm^2.' Is what Shane said correct?

Explain why to your friend.

> Investigate different polygons Shane could make with his 10 sticks.

2. Maeve's Parallelograms

Maeve draws 3 parallelograms on an 8×8 dotty grid.

Copy Maeve's 3 parallelograms.

Explain to a friend how you know that each is a parallelogram.

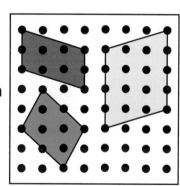

Maeve says, 'The area of my red parallelogram is 6 square units.'

Is what Maeve said correct?

Explain how you decided to your friend.

Work out the areas of Maeve's green and yellow parallelograms.

Explain to your friend how you worked them out.

> Investigate areas of different parallelograms on 8×8 dotty grids.

The 9 Problem-Solving Strategies

1 Look for the important words in the question

Write them down.
Underline them.
Make sure I know what to do.

2 Look for a pattern

Can I see something happening over and over again?
Will this help me solve the problem?

3 Have a go

Try an answer.
Does the answer make sense?

4 Use a table or chart

Would something like this help?

5 Use a drawing

Can I draw something about the problem?
Will this help me to find the answer?

6 Work backwards

Can I start at the end of the question to help work it out?
Will my answer work?

7 Try an easier problem

Can I change the numbers in the question to make it simpler?
Will this make finding the answer easier?

8 Make a model

Can I use paper or blocks to help me find the answer?
Can I use people to help me find the answer?

9 Think logically

Can I tell something about the answer straight away?
Can I get rid of answers that are not correct?

SAY NO TO BULLYING
NOBODY DESERVES TO BE BULLIED
TELL AN ADULT YOU CAN TRUST

This Anti-Bullying campaign is supported by the Department of Education and Skills with the co-operation of the Irish Educational Publishers Association